A Combat Medic's

Escapes and *Escapades*

Life's Fears Conquered

William J. Shier

B&M
37755 Pebble Pointe Ct.
Clinton Township, MI 48038

FIRST EDITION

Library of Congress Control Number: 2008941121

ISBN 978-0-615-23203-4

Acknowledgements
The Bay Voice article reprinted with permission.
Editing services provided by Kathy Ann Nussman and Pamela Wingerter.

Printed in the United States of America

To: My Fellow Citizens
of Clinton Twp.

Dedicated to my heros of

No Man's Land

The
Combat
Medic

Thanks
Bill Shea

ACKNOWLEDGEMENTS
ഓ ♋

Margo, my wife

All four of my children

Kathy Ann Nussman, editing

Holly Glackin, cover design and final layout

Carol MacKenzie, attorney

Pamela Wingerter, editing

Solutions in Design, initial typesetting/composition services

Members of the 253rd Medical Detachment

Thanks to all those who encouraged me

PREFACE

by Bill Shier

Events in the last three or four years have prodded many of the sixteen million members of the armed forces to come forward and tell their own personal stories before all is lost with our passing. Many of the different branches each faced their own D-Day. The Marines did not flee the beaches of Guadalcanal or Iwo Jima. The sailors could not back off their ships when the Kamikaze suicide planes dove into their midst, and the flight crews of the Air Force could not leave their aircraft as the flak got so thick you could walk on it.

No amount of fear could deter these service people from the path that led to many deaths and, consequently, victory for the rest of us.

This is my story that you are about to read. You will see how my patriotic feelings had to overcome my fears and the hellish nightmare that I endured.

I grew up in an urban area on the east side of Detroit. Looking back, I now realize how naive and lacking in worldly experience I, as an eighteen-year-old, had been. Somehow I believe that fate does guide each of us. It brought me through my own personal D-Day and made me one of the lucky ones to return home.

I. GROWING UP IN DETROIT

In peace, as a wise man, he should make suitable preparation for war.

৵ Horace

70 mm • The Global Perspective

Black Tuesday, October 29, 1929, the U.S. Stock Market crashed, creating one of the worst economic crises in history. Eventually, the hardships would be shared by every American, indeed, worldwide in scope—The Depression— was a formative decade.

8 mm • My Personal Perspective

My Personal Battle: Coming into Faith

I was brought into existence from ordinary circumstances. Every small daily occurrence somehow contributed to the final, but never complete, structure of my humanity. From the day of my birth in the winter of 1926 to the day of my induction, all things would come to matter, to shape the person I would become.

My twenty-year-old mother weighed less than one hundred pounds and struggled with my birth, as I weighed nearly ten pounds! My father had his problems trying to negotiate the foot of snow that had fallen the day before. Even with 30-inch wheels, the Ford coupe had trouble getting through the unplowed streets of Detroit. Still, my father continued on to his goal of picking up the midwife

Dirt road and voting booth on Detroit's east side circa 1925.

who would assist at my birth. The young father was a line worker at one of the many Brigg's plants on the east side of Detroit. I was named "William" after my father, but all through my years I would be known as "Bill." The day was Saturday, February 20, 1926.

Memories of my life began after my third birthday when my youngest brother was born in Flint, Michigan. I remember playing under his crib on a warm sunny day in the summer of 1929. My next memory was of a vacant neighborhood store with all the shelves and counters removed. The small apartment in the rear was our living quarters, and the front of the store was where my brother Jack and I would play.

When I reflect back on these times, it has occurred to me that the stock market had crashed, and our nice home was lost. In the spring of 1930, the family moved back to Detroit. We rented the first floor of a small bungalow on Georgia Street. Housing units were hard to find and times were so hard that another family lived in the finished upstairs attic. From this time on, I was able to recount many of the everyday occurrences in my life.

Our front porch faced an entire open block across Georgia Street that was a play field all the way to Van Dyke. At the far end toward St. Cyril street was Burroughs intermediate school that also used the play field. The park had all the swings, ball diamonds, sand pits, and game areas available to us. On the Fourth of July, we watched the fireworks while sitting on our front porch.

One of the other things to do was watching 8 mm movies. A neighbor boy who lived down six or seven houses toward Van Dyke had a projector. On Saturdays, when we could come up with the needed pennies, we would watch movies in the attic with all of the other neighborhood kids.

That September at age 4 1/2 years old, I started school. It was at Cooper Elementary about four blocks from my home. In my future years, I displayed some sense of being a bright boy, but didn't show it in my early childhood. The first day of school when the class was let out for recess, I missed the fact that this was just for play time and proceeded to race home to

Bill in front of his grandparent's house at 6748 Seneca, Detroit, Michigan
June 19, 1927

surprise my mother. The next day she marched me back to school. She asked the teachers to please keep an eye on me.

The remainder of my time at Cooper Elementary consisted of rolling on the floor mats or playing in little skits. In the summer of 1931, we had to move again. This time it was onto busy McClellan Avenue between Gratiot and Harper Avenue. This would be the center of my universe for the next four years.

On the corner of Seneca and the dirt covered Peter Hunt Street, Bill is behind his Aunt Margie
June 19, 1927

Everything was available to me within a three-block area. Out the back door to the alley and turning left towards Harper Avenue, there was the Rebel Creamery property. It consisted of a larger dirt storage lot for the milk wagons next to a very large barn. Inside were many stalls to house the horses that pulled the wagons. On the far side of the lot facing May Street, was the outlet store for the dairy products. Some of my time would be spent searching the alleys for discarded milk bottles that I could redeem for the two-cent deposit.

On weekends, when the stables were quiet and all the horses were in, my two brothers and I would climb onto the shed roof next to the barn. From here we could reach a second story window, and this would allow us to look down into the stalls to watch the horses being groomed and fed.

After a short stay, we were off to our next adventure. On the north corner of our street was Harper Avenue. There was an old open air fruit and vegetable market. It was appropriately called the Harper-McClellan Market. It kept the name even after it was closed in and became a grocery store.

Walking east on Harper after crossing May Street, one approached the farmers market. I could enter at one end of the long corrugated building and exit at the far end. One stall that always drew my attention had a 55-gallon drum of boiling water. It was used by the workers to de-feather sold chickens while the customers waited. The exit at the far end led to the alley behind Gratiot Avenue. This block contained the most interesting businesses.

I enjoyed the stores on this block for the next three years. The corner, I believe, had a family tavern and next to that was a Woolworth's. Then there was a Neisner's and a fabric store and finally the S.S. Kresge's. All the stores had front and back door entrances. This was great for playing games with the neighborhood kids. After the dime stores, came the jewel of the block, the Roosevelt Theatre. It was large, beautiful, and new and had first-run movies every week. The first time I went to the theater was to see Tarzan of the Apes.

This showing was a Saturday afternoon special that only cost me a nickel to get in. The normal charge was ten cents to see a film, so it was awhile before I became a regular customer.

Next to the theater entrance on the corner of May Street

was an elegant jewelry store. I do not recall going into the store, but I spent many moments staring into the showcase windows. I would cross May Street back to my block where a florist shop took up the entire corner. After the open lot came the dime novel store where my mother could trade in two used books for another used one.

On the corner of Gratiot and McClellan was the local watering hole for my father. It had one of those catchy names, but over the years I am now unable to recall it. On the opposite corner was Strebb's hardware store. It covered the entire corner with outdoor displays and parking.

The rest of the block heading downtown consisted of the formula, that being a bar, a cleaners, a confectionery store, and a family grocery business. On occasion there would be a pet store with kittens or puppies in the front windows to lure me in. At Burns Avenue, we would cross Gratiot to visit the Mark Twain Branch Library. On Saturday morning, a group of neighborhood kids would meet there for one hour of storytelling. The stories were not always from books, but sometimes were made up by the storyteller.

In the early 1930s, when Gratiot Avenue was widened from Mack Avenue to Harper Avenue, the library was the only building put on rollers and moved back to a new foundation. All of the other businesses were torn down for the widening. There were some exceptions, and these were the business locations with large front lawns. They included Sears & Roebuck at Van Dyke, the Dawn Theatre at Iroquois, and the Ivory Moving & Storage Co. at Fischer Street. The city just paved right over their front lawns. Most of the south side of Gratiot was left with many open spaces because the empty lots were too small to allow any building.

That September, 1931, I started the first grade at
Chandler Elementary School. It was a four or five-block
walk up McClellan past Gratiot Avenue. This was past
the White Castle hamburger stand, with only six stools.
When I crossed Shoemaker Street, I passed in front of the
Nativity Church complex. It had a high brick and iron grate
wall surrounding all of the buildings, except the Church
doors. Sometimes when I was passing the wall, I would see
children playing, and most were girls in the same checked
clothes. The guard nuns in their long black robes were
doing a good job of keeping them inside the wall.

The four years that I attended Chandler School were
uneventful. The basics in reading, writing, and math came
easily for me, but my acting in many plays and skits was
done poorly. This has moved me all my life to center any
activities or playing around the family. Even to this day
the family agenda remains the same. Our home became
the focal point for parties and family gatherings. This was
due to the fact that my mother was the oldest of thirteen
children and the first to get married. The New Year's Eve
parties were the highlights of our family talks.

After school started, my brothers and I did not get to
roam to our favorite neighborhood hangouts as often as in
the summer months. So now our playtime extended to the
attic or to the half basement. If it wasn't too cold, we would
use the garage as a bunkhouse.

It was during these years that my nightmares began.
If I had any before I was six or seven years old, I don't
recall. I look back to the time when they first appeared,
searching for a contributing factor. This was before we had

a radio or I was a regular at the movies. The main themes
of my nightmares were wildfires and fire engines by the
dozens, rushing back and forth in the night. Or I would
be floundering underwater in an Atlantis setting, but not
drowning. Other times I would be falling out of the sky,
but not off of anything or into anything. I would wake up
terrified and only tell my mother that I was having a bad
dream if she should ask about it.

While living on McClellan, my first sister, Mary Ann,
was born in December of 1932. The following year my
parents started buying the Detroit News on Sundays, where
I discovered the comics. In 1934, my dad purchased a
Philco floor model radio with short-wave capabilities. This
is when I started listening to the Detroit Tigers baseball
games.

In the summer of 1935, the family was forced to move
again. This time it was to 8909 Peter Hunt Street at the
corner of Rohns Street. This small bungalow had three tiny
bedrooms and two little closets. Another family occupied
the attic, using an outside stairway for access. In the half-
basement lived another couple, whose job it was to watch
the property for the owner. Times must have been tough
because my parents rented the second bedroom to a fellow
from Ohio who worked with my dad.

The school this time was A. L. Holmes, just two blocks
away. The school was a completely enclosed building with
a large courtyard used for parking cars and delivery trucks.
To get into this area, a section of the first floor had a part
removed for the driveway. At this point the hallway took a
half rise over the driveway and then a half dip back down. I
was at this school for only three months because the house

was sold, and we had to move again.

My grandparents, that had been renting just five blocks away, bought this house in December of 1935. We moved three miles up Rohns Street to an old, empty house owned by a great aunt of my mother's. This time my parents also bought to keep from moving in the near future.

Our next home at 4446 Rohns Street in Detroit should have accepted a no-bid contract to have it bulldozed long before it was purchased by my parents. Even at ten years of age, I could see what a giant patching job was needed just to make the place livable. The plastered walls and the ceiling had cracks the size of the Grand Canyon. The floors were warped and worn beyond repair. Most of the windows were painted shut, and the only redeeming factor of this place was it kept us out of the elements.

Everything in the house was pre-WWI, such as the wood stove in the dining room and the ancient hot water tank next to the kitchen sink. The first thing my father did was seal the walls to keep out the cold winds and buy yards of linoleum to cover all of the floors.

In the twenty-three plus years that my parents lived here, they made many changes and other improvements. With two brothers and two sisters, the sleeping arrangements were awkward and tight for space. My sisters got the one small first floor bedroom, and my parents slept in the sitting room off the living room. My two brothers and I slept in one half of the attic that had been finished with nailed-on cardboard. The house had a half basement where my mother would do the laundry (after my father moved the hot water tank from the kitchen). An outside stairway was used to go downstairs, but it did have a cover over it. The winters were the toughest for me because the only heat in the attic was from an open grate over the dining room stove.

In January of 1936, my brothers and I started the new year at Pingree Elementary School. We were here only for a half term because in September we transferred to St. Catherine's parochial school. This was a new experience for me, but one thing remained the same. I was not readily accepted into any groups, which made me withdraw even further into myself.

Moves and changes in my life did not alter my recurring nightmares. Although I did not realize it at the time, my nightmares were about to dissolve and disappear. In my second year at St. Catherine's, I made my First Communion. I am unable to explain this, having been only eleven years old at the time.

One of the new things in my life was how I became intrigued with music. I loved to dance and sing along with jazz and swing music on the radio in those early years. As I grew older into my teens, I was still withdrawn and lived life as a loner. In today's world, I would be considered the "complete nerd." So now my nightmares are gone, but they are replaced by my daydreams.

With any money I received or later earned with my paper route, I used to go to the movies. By the time I was fifteen years old, I was at the show five or six times a week. Looking back at these times, I wonder if things would have improved by my using some of the money to change my appearance.

To save money, my mother dressed my brother and me with hand-me-down clothes. It was a rare day when we would have something new to wear. One incident that still stands out in my memory occurred when I was fifteen years old in my freshman year of high school. Although I begged for a pair of long pants, I was told that there wasn't money for this. So I continued to wear my uncle's old golf knickers to class. This just embarrassed me to tears as I could hear the snickers behind my back.

As the school years faded into the past, I was included in some of the classroom discussions and activities. This came about because of a few classmates who had been with me all the way into high school. This did not extend out of school, but by the tenth grade, I would go to some of the basketball or football games with the class. The away-from-home games that I was able to attend were more enjoyable because somehow I didn't feel as alone. If I had been more at ease with my appearance and confident in my abilities, I should have joined the choir because of my love of singing. This probably would have helped with my dancing, too.

When school ended during the summer of 1942, my mother asked me to quit my paper route. She wanted me to get a job to enable me to contribute money towards my room and board.

The Early War Months

This new direction for me, going into the work force, seemed like the ideal change. There were many jobs available because so many of the young men had been drafted at the beginning of World War II. The first newspaper ad that I called and interviewed for hired me. I lasted four months at this job, but do not remember why I left it in September of 1942. My mother asked me if I was going to return to high school or continue to work.

Well, she did not have to ask me that because I still did not want to be an outsider at school. (Today I know that I should have shown a stiff upper lip and continued with my education.)

I wandered from one menial job to the next for eighteen months until I was called up for military service. It never occurred to me that my lack of education prevented me from obtaining a real job. I continued to live in my dream world, spending all of my time at the theater watching movies or live bands. During this time, I was fortunate to see all of the major swing bands, and when I left the shows, I would be singing into the air with gusto with only myself listening or even caring.

At the last two places I worked, there were young people that hung out together after work. This allowed me to join in as a loner, being it was not a couple's thing. I also started buying more attractive clothing and spending on personal grooming for myself. My physical appearance improved as I got older. Plus at sixteen, I shot up over a foot in height.

My spiritual life was at a hit or miss stage, but my moral sense was still firm and unchanged. There was nothing going on in my life, but this period was about to close. Now that I was about to reach draft age, a new and more exciting story of my life would evolve.

The Small War: A Personal Chapter

The first thing I remember uttering to myself about WWII was in September of 1939 when Poland was invaded. I was thirteen years old at the time and said this would be over way before I would be involved in it. I was thankful for that because I was a quiet and introverted teen, unable to kill the smallest of bugs or rodents. My prayers became more fervent now, because there was no way I wanted to kill anything, especially humans.

Five years passed, and on my eighteenth birthday in 1944, I registered for the draft. A few weeks later the first of many notices arrived. Report for a physical on Saturday, April 1st at the old warehouse at McDougall and E. Larned in Detroit, Michigan, which after WWII became the University of Detroit Dental School with an entrance on Jefferson.

The day arrived with me taking the Crosstown streetcar to Cadillac where I transferred to a bus that traveled on E. Congress. The bus stopped only a block from the warehouse, making it a short walk for me. All of us were herded through the many stations on each floor.

First check was the eyes, then the ears, and then the heart for high blood pressure. When the medic took mine, his eyes lit up, and he signaled for help to get me to a cot in another room. My pressure was 210 over 120, and they assumed that two hours on a cot would bring it down to a satisfactory level.

All of this time, we are all stark naked to speed up the exams of which hemorrhoids seemed to be the most important, and don't forget to turn your head and cough at the right time. Well, that's all over, and I passed with flying colors "they said."

The next choice was mine alone. Did I want the army, navy, or the marines, but I was not giving up that easily.

After dressing, I was ready to give my answer, but instead I blurted out, "It's April Fools' Day! Surely you were kidding when you said I had passed, and you're in the army now."

II. LEAVING DETROIT

It's what you learn after you know it all that counts.

❧ John Woods

70 mm

Early 1944, preparations are well underway for the invasion of France. D-Day. The war in Africa was over; Italy was being liberated, and in the Pacific, the direction of the war was now clear: fighting to the end, Japan was losing.

8 mm

Getting the Call

Thirty days passed till May 1, 1944. I received my notice to report in ten days to Ft. Sheridan, Illinois. On Thursday, the 11th, I was escorted by my father to the Michigan Central Depot for my first train ride to Chicago, Illinois.

From Union Station, the recruits were led to the Inter Urban for the final leg of the trip to Ft. Sheridan, Illinois. All of the recruits were met by army cadre and were marched into camp and the temporary barracks to be used for just one night. Since it was late, the recruits were told to get a meal at the mess hall, and swearing in would be the next morning.

That night I lay in the upper bunk with my clothes on because that was all I had with me. Before I drifted off to sleep, I heard sobbing in all areas of the barracks that night.

Friday, May 12th turned out to be the day the other recruits and I would say "I do" to Uncle Sam. This was done in a large gym where quick physicals and shots were given prior to the reading of the Articles of War and then raising your right hand to accept your fate.

The next three days were spent taking tests, eating three meals a day, and keeping the barracks clean. I did learn I had passed in the upper 20 percent on the IQ test. On the morning of the 16th of May, all were ordered to gather all personal and issue items before the march to a waiting train and a long three-day ride to Camp Hood, Texas. The old troop train was a tooth rattler, and a black cloud of ash from the ancient engine filled all the cars with a thick layer of soot.

III. ENTERING THE ARMY

Loyalty must arise spontaneously from the heart of people who love their country and respect their government.

ง Justice Hugo Black

70 mm

Bill Shier, Fort Sheridan, Illinois May 1944

In total secret, the United States had been preparing to end the war as quickly as possible. The Manhattan Project had been underway for several years — developing "the bomb."

8 mm

The Start of Basic Training

On the third day of this uneventful, really boring trip, I arrived at Camp Hood, Texas. Thursday, May 18, 1944, and it was the beginning of one of the hottest summers in Texas history. The troops arrived wearing their winter uniforms and struggled to march into the camp without collapsing from the heat.

Basic training began early the next morning. We were up at 6:00 a.m., straightening out our bunks and the immediate area after washing up and dressing. We then assembled outside to be counted. After a quick thirty

Camp Hood, Texas.
July 1944

minutes of calisthenics, we headed to breakfast in the mess hall. I was assigned to Company B, 159th Bn., 73rd Regiment. We had fifty-six men in the 4th platoon using one barrack, and I got myself a top bunk close to a heater vent because, believe it or not, the nights were on the chilly side after 110 degrees in the daytime.

Classes followed breakfast starting with rifle nomenclature, map reading, and plane identification until lunchtime. In the afternoon, there was backpacking, marching at close quarters, and field calisthenics that included every obstacle course. This meant staying out of the water hole by not letting go of the rope. Each week, one or two recruits took a nosedive into the dirt because of the extreme heat and the tough training.

Just two and a half weeks into basic training on Tuesday, we were on our way to lunch when word reached us that D-Day, the 6th of June, had occurred. Before one could snap one's fingers, all were whooping it up and cheering, for the thinking was that the war would end before the week was out.

Getting Tough in Texas

Well, so much for the short-lived celebration. We endured the first four weeks of basic, and we started our antitank training on 37 mm guns and a few hours a day at the pistol and rifle range, learning firsthand about our firepower.

The heat of the summer in Texas intensified, leading to more heat strokes, and I broke out in heat rash that has stayed with me to this day. Everything in July and August was planned as much as possible in some sort of shade. More of our forced marches were during the evening, which was scary because our earlier daytime marches were on the back roads of these 2400 square miles where wildlife was abundant. We chased armadillos, kicked large tarantulas at our feet, and watched as jack rabbits headed for cover. On one of the earlier night hikes, I was taking my ten-minute break, lying on a rock formation and staring at the heavens filled with a million glittering stars, when a scorpion stung me in the neck. I was momentarily paralyzed, but managed to regain my movement after several minutes, and continued on the march.

The direction of this new stage finds me going headlong into the unknown, but looking back, I now believe there was a spiritual being guiding my every action. How could I make so many good moves and just as many bad moves, but escape to the same situation every day and sometimes for even months.

The daily training routine toughened up all of the men in my company. All of the exercises benefit body and mind, but there were times in the field where I must have goofed at a particular exercise. More than once I was referred to as "Joe Doaks" by someone from my platoon. As in grade school and in high school, I never got close to or hung out with any of my fellow servicemen.

All through basic training, my only thoughts were of surviving this grueling endurance test. No thoughts of home and loved ones, no thoughts of Church and God. No thoughts of how I was going to do this, but just pressing onward. This was probably in the back of my mind and did not let me seek out any friendships.

To break up the three-and-a-half months at Camp Hood, I spent as much time as possible at the canteen club where live bands performed on weekends with lots of dancing to watch. One of the regulars was Johnny Scat Davis, and there were also many appearances of the popular female vocalists of the day as well.

Basic Completed

At the end of August and the beginning of September 1944, my fellow warriors and I completed our schoolroom and book training. The warlike maneuvers and living in the field began: sleeping in cold and wet tents, crawling through the mud to avoid machine gun fire over our heads, enjoying meals from trucks, and eating off our tin trays. I was kidding about the enjoying part because "war is hell," and the rest of the next twelve months would prove it to be true.

With the completion of the field exercises, I returned to camp to pack up for the two weeks furlough at home. Captain Baker commended everyone for completing the training and posed for the company picture with us and the cadre. I want to note it here that these draftees were from locations that had depleted the availability of young men to call up for service. One recruit was blind in one eye; another had one short leg, and another was thirty-seven years old, weighed 125 pounds, plus had seven children at home. Some others were older than I, being in their late twenties and early thirties, but all of these persevered and were honored for completing basic training. All received their assignments along with their furlough papers.

After spending my time at home with my family, I headed for Centreville, Mississippi, to join the 63rd Division as a medical replacement. God had answered my prayers because now I would not have to carry a weapon of death.

Joining the Division

The new adventure for me was all the train rides on my own. My first was going home after basic training and then returning to duty at Camp Van Dorn, Mississippi. As the train left Chicago, I found a seat next to a beautiful young woman by the name of Jean, who was from Butler, Pennsylvania, and was seventeen years old, but engaged to a soldier near a New Orleans camp. Although I was introverted and very shy, I managed to befriend Jean before we parted in Jackson, Mississippi. I exchanged a few letters with her before I shipped out for overseas duty, but never heard from her again.

The train stopped at McComb, Mississippi, where I picked up a bus to complete my journey to Camp Van Dorn at Centreville. My assignment was as an aidman working with an ambulance driver. For the next six weeks, work consisted of first aid training and learning the anatomy, plus some overnight field trips where I would sleep in the ambulance if no one was checking.

The recreation around this camp consisted of storytelling, which included how several soldiers died on bivouac when bitten by coral snakes that had crawled into their sleeping bags. Other stories dwelled on all of the deserters that numbered in the hundreds, including several officers and even a chaplain. Early in November of 1944, the 63rd Division packed and boarded a train for a POE location in upstate New York.

Riding the Troop Train

The trip to the POE was my fifth long train ride during the past seven months. The division left Mississippi and traveled through Alabama, then turned north to Tennessee and Kentucky. At night, when the bunks were made up, I'd lie there staring out the window, gazing at the city lights that passed before my eyes. As usual, the troop train spent a lot of time on sidings to let high priority trains get past our car. At this rate, it took more than two days to travel to Camp Shanks just north of New York City.

Camp Shanks was a small camp on top of a medium-sized Appalachian peak overlooking the Hudson River. The railroad followed the Hudson River's path right into Penn Station in Manhattan, New York. Our activities at camp were minimal, just enough to keep us busy until the other troops and I would be heading for the New York Harbors.

On Monday, November 13, 1944, when I was supposed to be out around camp keeping busy and fit, I went back to my barracks instead. One of the Division officers was inspecting the barracks and found me asleep in my bunk. He marched me off to the commandant's office to report my actions. I was ordered restricted to the immediate barracks area to haul firewood and keep up the stove fires for the rest of our stay at Camp Shanks.

The Last Furlough to New York City

On Thursday, November 16, 1944, the Officer of the Day ordered me to check with all personnel in our group to see who would like to make one last trip into New York City. After checking with everyone, I was returning the list to the company office when I decided to add my name to the list. To my complete surprise, being under discipline, a pass for me was available the next morning, so I took off for New York.

Upon arrival at Penn Station, I looked for directions to the nearest YMCA to reserve a bed for that night. My next stop was at the St. Nicholas Club on West 48th Street, looking for tickets to Friday and Saturday shows or parties. One of my choices was the Victory Center on West 42nd Street and the U.S.O. dance late in the evening.

On Saturday, I visited Rockefeller Center and the RCA Building where I had the opportunity to get on a television transmission that appeared on trial TV sets around the building. Throughout this entire weekend, I don't remember when I ate or slept. Saturday night I had a ticket for the Lincoln Square Center where the Dick Gates Orchestra started playing after 8:30 p.m. My stay here lasted just over an hour when some of the other servicemen said to try the dance at Hunter's College. It was being held at the Roosevelt House in Upper Manhattan. This was a beautiful old stone mansion that the Roosevelt family loaned to the college for these special occasions and dances.

There were dozens of young ladies, so beautiful that the

mere sight of them took my breath away! I was introduced
to one striking lady with whom I chatted for some time.
But, true to form, I was too timid to ask her for a dance.
So Bess Myerson, who was Miss America of 1945, moved
on to talk with some of the other servicemen. Once again,
my shyness arose, and another opportunity for a golden
memory was forever lost.

The Surprise Back at Camp

On Sunday, I returned to Broadway visiting the different
clubs and theaters. I checked out the Jack Dempsey Bar
and went up to the top of the Empire State Building, then
watched the skaters at Rockefeller Center ice rink. In the
late afternoon I caught the train back to Camp Shanks,
and when I reached the gates—what a surprise! My squad
leader and the platoon sergeant were waiting for me, and I
was quickly escorted to the company headquarters.

Major Carlson and two other officers were across the
table from me. They informed me that I was being court-
martialed for desertion and asked me what I had to say on
my behalf. I explained that I had a pass signed by the Major,
giving me permission to leave camp. They looked at me with
quizzical faces, and one officer stammered that I was told to
stay in camp and should have honored the verbal order.

My reply was that in a few months, I could be killed,
and I had decided to take my chances with one last fling in
New York City.

The final outcome of my general court-martial on
November 19, 1944, was that I was a deserter, but I would
return to my company and ship out when they left on the
following week. Nothing was ever said to me again about

this day, and I do not even know it if was included in my service records.

The following Thursday, November 23rd, was the one time in our history that Americans had two Thanksgiving dinners. The first was for the Republicans, and the second was for the Roosevelt Democrats, which is still used to this day — the last Thursday of November.

The Convoy Leaves New York

On the day following Thanksgiving, I, along with the rest of the Division, packed up and boarded the train for New York Harbor. At the dock, I boarded the S.S. Thomas H. Barrie, which held the 253rd Regiment Headquarters Group. The balance of the regimental group was boarded on the S.S. Sea Robin, including the medical detachment.

The S.S. Thomas H. Barrie was a converted prewar Caribbean cruise ship by the name of Oriete that had, among its other luxuries, a small hospital section that included two small rooms with four bunk beds in each of them. The balance of the Division was on other troop ships that made up the total convoy.

We sailed out into the Atlantic the next morning where the entire convoy assembled into formation and proceeded to head south the first day. A large portion of land lovers and I were seasick the first couple days, but the bunk bed held me fast and saved my stomach until I was able to maneuver out on deck.

The convoy passed by Bermuda, then swung east across the middle Atlantic. Our entire stay on board the ship was to last fourteen days. Six days out to sea, I had my second Thanksgiving dinner on November 30th, 1944. It was served to me on a large divided tray that I carried to a high bar table where we stood to eat because there wasn't a chair or stool in sight. Thank goodness, I was over the seasickness and enjoyed every bite of turkey and trimmings.

The Crossing

As the convoy approached the Canary Islands, our ship pulled away in a big circle followed by one of the destroyer escorts. The S.S. Thomas H. Barrie met up with a merchant ship for refueling that took several hours to complete.

I watched from the stern of the ship with others and quizzed a seaman about being separated from the rest of the convoy. I was told that a convoy only travels about nine knots an hour, and the S.S. Thomas H. Barrie would catch up easily, doing 28 knots an hour. This speed also helped the ship to outrun any subs that might come into the area.

We caught up to the convoy just as we were passing the Straits of Gibraltar where the lights of the city of Algiers were visible to us. The last two days were spent going through the Mediterranean Sea until we passed Corsica, then made a left turn north, headed to Marseille, France. We entered the harbor late afternoon on December 7, 1944, and waited until the next morning to disembark.

My walk down the gangplank was with mixed emotions, and the dreariness of the day did not help to calm my fears of my first steps on foreign soil. I carried my heavy duffel bag to a waiting 2 1/2-ton army truck that was to transport the Division to a rural mountaintop north of the city. It was called the Delta Staging Area where we would wait until the entire Division assembled before moving to the front lines.

IV. WAR IN EUROPE

War is cruel and you cannot refine it.

∾ William Tecumseh Sherman, 1864

70 mm

While the world anxiously awaits the Normandy Invasion and the liberation of Paris, almost unnoticed, the Allies invade southern France to open a third front against the Wehrmacht. Cornered on three sides, the Germans begin to crumble.

19th Birthday. Alsace-Lorraine, France
February 20, 1945

8 mm

The Division on the Move

M y fellow medics and I sat on top of a stone mountain, doing nothing but attempting to keep busy. I had a week of cold and wet miseries without a building, a cave, or a tent to get comfortable in during the bleak daytime hours. At night I crawled into two large cardboard boxes I found in the nearby railroad yard. It was cramped inside the box, and I was unable to fully stretch out inside my sleeping bag. Of course, this was better than attempting to erect a pup tent when the pegs would not pierce the rock on which I was resting.

The time came on Friday, December 15th, when the entire 253rd Regiment was loaded on trucks and some very old 40x8 railroad boxcars, designated 40x8 because they would hold either 40 people or 8 horses. We were squeezed into the boxcar until all forty were aboard and our duffle bags stacked at each end of the boxcar. My miseries continued to mount being in these unheated boxcars in mid-December with no sanitary facilities, so I did without and made do with whatever.

During daylight hours, stops were made to eat, stretch, and relieve ourselves. At night we had to lie on our sides and face each other to have enough room for all forty to lie down to get some sleep. Those in front of the sliding doors had even more misery when a GI needed to relieve himself by crawling on top of everyone and then have the spray blow back into their faces. A couple of hours into the first night, I got off the floor and climbed on top of the duffle bags at one end of the boxcar and found the lumpy bags much better for sleeping.

Arriving at Camp Number Two

I spent two days and two nights on this leg of my odyssey. The one good thing that I liked on this ride was joining a group to form a singing quartet. We spent many hours harmonizing at night for as long as possible to avoid going to sleep.

On day three, December 17, 1944, the Regiment arrived at Camp Oberhoffen, France. Weeks before I arrived in France, this camp held a German garrison, but now it was

completely abandoned and unoccupied. The bunk bed that
I was assigned still had the old straw mattress on it, which
I covered with my bedroll. We spent two nights at this
camp, then were moved up to Roppenheim, France, where
the medics stayed, and the balance of the Regiment set up
camp at Munchausen and Neuhaeusel, France. I was at this
location for one week until the 29th of December. It was
on the Rhine River, and the Germans occupied the east side
of the river. On Christmas night, I could look across the
river and make out the German campfires as well as hear
them singing Christmas carols. I thought to myself, "What
a crazy war."

On Christmas day, the Catholic chaplain came around
to see if any of us wanted to attend Christmas mass. I
said, "Yes, I would like that," and so did PFC Dekever
who walked with me to the Catholic Church in town. The
chaplain and his jeep driver, who doubled as altar boy,
Dekever, and I made up what must have been one of the
smallest services attended in history.

Moving to a New Front

On the 29th of December, 1944, the regiment motored
back to Camp Oberhoffen for a couple of days to regroup,
and then on New Year's Eve, we moved to Oermimgem,
France. I was at this location for three days, then on to
Sarreguemines, France. Sarreguemines is located in Alsace-
Lorraine but farther up the Sarre River, which I learned
many years later was the home of my family forefathers
until 1709 when they migrated to Limerick, Ireland. The
war at this moment seemed to be in limbo with no action
anywhere along this front. The civilians were returning, and

DeKever, Bill Shier, Carey, Plattner, Scherf (facing away), Spaeter, a civilian
Alsace-Lorraine, France February 1, 1945

the city had some semblance of normalcy with some stores and shops opening up.

I found a photography shop open and had a posed photo of myself in wartime uniform taken for my nineteenth birthday that was the following month. Unknown to me at this time was the fact that Sarreguemines was the jumping off point into Germany on our final push to subdue the enemy. These past weeks were the last tokens of tranquility I would have to relish until the end of the war in Europe.

Of course, there were some isolated moments of excitement within my squad. As medics, we usually commandeered some large home to stay in and use it as living quarters as well as a field medical office. Being the low man on the totem pole, I was assigned the fireplace

Werick, Archer, Carey, a civilian, Spaeter, Shier, Scherf, Plattner, DeKever

Alsace-Lorraine, France, February 1, 1945

duty, but never being a boy scout, I did not know how to start fires. I loaded these massive stone fireplaces with paper and wood and poured on gasoline. I was lucky enough to survive two large explosions that shook the entire mansion. Clearly, I was not learning my lesson.

Germany Invaded

At 3:00 a.m. on February 16, 1945, the squad leader came into our second floor sleeping area and informed us to get out of our sleeping bags, for it was time to push off. This is where emotions kick into action as excitement and fear clashed within me, but as I learned in the coming months, it is better when our instincts are followed. I had to push fear aside at all times in order not to paralyze myself

Werick, Archer, Carey, Bill Shier, Spaeter, Scherf, Plattner, DeKever

Alsace-Lorraine, France, February 1, 1945

or look cowardly. This probably was the norm for all of the GI's on this mission to free all people.

I was assigned as the balance of one litter-bearing squad and one field medic to B Company of the 253rd Regiment for the day's action. I was the very last person in the single-line procession crossing the Sarre River on a hastily constructed pontoon bridge. We felt our way along in the darkness on the German side of the river, scrambled up the embankment to our destination, the railroad tracks.

We bypassed Hanweiler, Germany, and walked the tracks farther into enemy territory. I was cautioned to step on each tie and not in between, as that was where the foot mines were planted. The darkness at 4:00 a.m. was bad enough to slow us down, but there was also low-lying fog

Carey, Bill Shier, Spaeter, Scherf, Plattner, DeKever, behind are Werick, Archer

Alsace-Lorraine, France, February 1, 1945

with which to contend. My nearsightedness was a large problem, and I was falling behind the column. Now my fear was really growing. I thought I might lose the entire company in front of me and be left in this foreign land by myself. I struggled to move along faster by bending over with my face closer to the railroad ties, hoping for a quick dawn light. One hour into the march, I noticed a spot with a rail tie missing. I attempted to step to the outside of the rail to avoid the hole in the rail bed. This was a bad move! This I later learned when I regained consciousness from my fall into a small, dry riverbed below the tracks. Now I was really terrified as I scrambled up the bank to get back onto the tracks above me. I had lost my helmet, and I don't know what else. All I wanted now was to catch up to my fellow troops as soon as possible. I raced across the rail ties in a desperate mind set, not caring if I stayed on the ties or in between. If I did not catch up, I would be dead anyway. After an hour or so I spotted the last man in the column which happened to be from the litter-bearing squad. He didn't even know I was missing. About 6:00 a.m., a sliver of light appeared on the horizon, but also an eerie fog still lay low over the tracks, giving us some cover. Not for long, as gunfire soon erupted. The entire company dove down between the tracks for some protection.

With my helmet gone, I grabbed a 30-caliber ammo canister to hold over my head. Yet another dumb move on my part as the ammo canister was full, and one direct shot would have taken my head off. Machine gun fire raked over us for a half hour or so until a squad moved in from the flank and captured the location.

The Encirclement Begins

The infantry company left the tracks and headed in to form a large circle, cutting off all of the German troops back to the Sarre River. Within the next hour that morning, my litter squad was given our first call to pick up a wounded GI at the new front line. He was lifted onto our litter, and I grabbed a handle on the back as all four of us picked him up to start the long trek back to the aid station. I was exhausted before one hour had gone by. The four of us would rush for thirty or forty feet, then set the litter down for a few minutes. We attempted to move along the same area that was covered by the advancing troops.

Scherf, Bill Shier, Capt. Whelon, Sgt. Carey
Alsace-Lorraine, France, February 1, 1945

Unfortunately, this was high and open ground. The next thing I knew, we were spotted by German mortar gunners who had us zeroed in with two quick shots. Before the third round landed, we were up and running again, and the spot where we were resting became a big crater. I ran with the rest of the team till we all dropped with exhaustion again. The German gunners were still on us, and again two rounds landed even closer. In terror, we leaped up again to clear the spot we were resting in before round three hit.

This continued for nearly a quarter mile till we cleared the open area and got back into the woods nearby. All of the time that I was carrying this 200-pound plus Iowan farm boy, he was pleading with us to just set him down and save ourselves. Through all of his pain from his wounds that wouldn't even let him walk, he could see the agony and pain in our faces as we struggled to save him.

When we returned to the railroad tracks, we were over halfway back to the footbridge where we would cross back into France and the waiting ambulance for our wounded GI.

I later learned that it took us six hours to cover 2 1/2 miles to save our patient, and for this I, along with the rest of the litter squad, was awarded the Bronze Star. A follow-up note to this adventure occurred when a second infantry company coming up the tracks to support Company B found my helmet with the large Red Cross painted on it, picked it out of the river bed, and returned it to me when told of my losing it that morning.

After the division gained a hold on the German side of the river, our 253rd Regiment pushed to the Siegfried Line. We busted through with little opposition, taking several weeks to do so.

My next adventure was in St. Ingbert, Germany, where we set up the next aid station. The following morning I walked to the center of the city and looked around at the different stores and homes that were still intact, but deserted. I entered one nice looking home on main street and went from empty room to empty room. In a back bedroom, there was a chest of drawers all by itself which I did not look into, but did notice something on a shelf in the closet. There were two albums, each containing one hundred photos with a special kaleidoscope lens in a sliding holder. The photos and lens were in pockets made in the front and back covers with one slot for the viewing lens. A story explaining each photo was in the middle of each album.

I picked up both albums plus some photos that were loose without any cover, put them under my arm and headed back to the aid station. I was again reminded by the sergeant that picking up souvenirs was dangerous because of all the booby trap mines that Germans left behind. Not one hour later a wounded GI was brought in with both hands missing. He told us that he was looking for souvenirs in town when he went into a nice home that still had a chest of drawers in the bedroom. When he went to open one of the drawers, it blew up in his face taking his hands off. I knew then that I had a guardian angel, and I was protected from this disaster.

In the coming weeks, the other medics and I had many calls into the no man's land of this war. Some of our calls were routine, but others were the horrors endured by many in the line of duty. The calls at night made my blood run cold almost every time. On one such run, I had to lie on the hood of the jeep, and with only the dim light of the slits over the head lamps, I was supposed to look for land mines in the road or land depressions to avoid. If they had known how bad my eyesight was, I'm sure they would have chosen another for this job.

Carrying on My Job

The next real challenge for my guardian angel occurred on a call where the wounded GI was in a foxhole some ten yards into no man's land. Across the quarter-mile field, lay more woods filled with German troops and tanks.

The other three medics in my litter squad and I crawled out to the foxhole on our stomachs, dragging the litter behind us. When we attempted to lift the wounded GI out of the foxhole, he let out one hell of a scream. We quickly pulled on him to get the GI out and set him on a litter just as fast as possible, then started running for the protection of the woods behind us.

Within minutes, German 88 mm gunfire tore into the treetops above us. His scream had been heard across the meadow, and the Germans opened fire from their tanks. We all dove for the ground in front of us, leaving the poor wounded GI on the litter next to us. I was so sure that this was my final hour that I took a small prayer book from my pocket and proceeded to read it, although my face was only inches from the ground.

After what seemed like hours, but was probably no more than fifteen or twenty minutes, the barrage ended. When I looked up, the entire forest of trees around me was blown off at the top. I then stood up and looked down at the ground where I was lying. In a near perfect outline on the ground was a line of splintered wooden spikes from two to five feet long. It looked like a chalk outline of a murder victim. I just could not believe that there were so many splinters and not one hit any of us.

Once again we picked up our wounded patient and carried him to our jeep on a road behind the woods. We strapped him on the hood and jumped into the jeep for our ride back to the aid station.

A Step Away from Tragedy

The last two weeks of March 1945 were spent in a fast-paced chase of the retreating Germans. I had minimal work in the field on my ride to the Rhine River. Early one morning, the aid station received a call to pick up another wounded GI in an area inaccessible to our jeep. The litter team did get a ride to a trail close to a high ridge from which we started to walk. The four of us climbed this slightly wooded ridge up about twenty to thirty feet high and slid down the other side to a large open meadow. We all spread out to look for signs of where the forward troops were as we marched across this meadow. We gained the woods on the other side and continued on for another thirty minutes or so before coming across the forward position of our 253rd Regiment. They directed us to our patient, and we proceeded to load him onto our litter.

After a few minutes of rest, we picked up the GI and started back through the woods and the meadow beyond. The four of us again struggled with the long haul and the heavy load. We stopped often to rest and catch our breath. As we exited the woods, what we saw in front of us really shook us up. The company engineers had come up behind us, clearing the area for land mines. The entire meadow was crisscrossed with white tape showing where each land mine was located.

We explained that just hours before that we had come that way on our mission of mercy. We were told that might be so, but that we would have to go around the meadow through the white taped corridor the engineers had staked out. To this day, I am unable to understand how the other three members of the team and I did not set off one of the land mines.

We safely made the ridge and started our climb up with the GI on the litter. Halfway up, I somehow twisted my ankle and dropped to my knees. I struggled to keep the litter level and the patient on it. The other team members lowered their corners quickly to keep all of us from rolling back down to the bottom of the ridge. After a few minutes rest, I was able to step on the foot, although still in some pain. We practically slid the litter down the far side of the ridge to the waiting jeep that drove us safely back to the aid station. I was able to rest my ankle for a couple of days before our next move to the front lines.

The countryside in this area was hilly and had some small mountainous locations that we had to march through. In one such small village, a row of houses was next to the road on each side and a second row of houses higher up the hillside.

As we neared the halfway point through the village, gunfire came at us from the second row of houses on the left side. I dove to a deep gutter on my left to seek cover while the troops at the front of the column swung quickly to the left side. They circled to the rear of the houses to flush out the Germans who were still raking us with gunfire and a few German grenades, called potato mashers. One of the grenades rolled to the edge of the sidewalk near my head and exploded. The shrapnel bounced off my helmet, leaving a ringing in my ears for several hours. Soon we had the all clear and continued our march.

Heidelberg: The Open City

We arrived at Heidelberg, Germany on April 1, 1945, Easter Sunday. Before entering the city, all the troops were informed that there would be no shooting in the city. That was an agreement reached on both sides that Heidelberg had been designated as an open city.

We learned that the city had a medical college and many of the students were German soldiers in uniform as well as workers at the school. I spent the day looking over the city in our immediate area. The streets had many civilians out shopping, and they stared at us, and we stared right back at them. This was really an awkward situation for me, and I thought to myself, "War is hell, but this is really crazy."

This break gave me a chance to clean up and get my supplies ready for the next day's push farther into Germany.

Heidelberg, West Germany
April 1, 1945

The next morning as we pulled out of Heidelberg, I noticed some of the jeeps and 3/4-ton trucks with their trailers were weaving and moving erratically. Later that day information filtered down to us that some of our troops had raided several wineries and replaced the trailer supplies with their hoard of ill-gotten brews. The drunken drivers and many others, including several officers and noncoms, were busted to a lower rank and chastised for their actions

The Final Two Weeks of My War: Giving up the Fight

For the next two weeks, our medical group spent our time following the fast-moving companies, just chasing the Germans with very few casualties. The weather was improving every day, making the fighting easier for us.

Early on Monday morning, April 16, Sgt. Archer informed us that we had to leave right after breakfast to find Company B to pick up a wounded GI. The litter team moved into the jeep around 9:00 a.m., and to my surprise, the sergeant and 1st Lt. Jordan joined us. With the driver, Cpl. Phillips, this made seven of us crowded into the jeep on this run for another pickup.

The area was heavily forested and mountainous, and I hoped the driver knew where he was going because I was completely lost in this foreign countryside. We were moving quickly along a narrow blacktopped road through the woods when we came upon a large home that was several hundred feet off to our right side. For some reason, the driver pulled to a quick stop. The reason, it turned out to be, was the sight of four or five German soldiers washing up in a watering trough near the house. They were half dressed, and as soon as they spotted us, they all dashed into the house. Our short-lived conversation was that the medics were about to take some more German prisoners. To our surprise, the German soldiers came running out of the house followed by the rest of their army squad.

Traveling in style—a 1936 Mercedes-Benz 540K Cabriolet C Special—didn't make being a POW any easier

They all were carrying automatic weapons and were blasting away at us. In unison we all leaped from the jeep to the ditch on our left side. Miraculously, no one was hit, but Sgt. Archer did get skinned as one bullet passed between his legs and another between his nose and the glasses he was wearing. When the barrage ended, the jeep was almost cut in half from the hail of fire. The Germans called out to us to surrender, so I put my hands on my head and marched out of the ditch with the other six medics.

The war was winding down, and I could think of no reason for the Germans to keep us alive. I don't know what the others were thinking, but I was so terrified that it's a wonder I didn't have a stroke due to my high blood pressure.

In a short time, the German soldiers had gathered their things and readied us to march farther to the rear, but before we left, they had Cpl. Phillips pull the jeep under the trees to hide it from aerial view.

We entered the small village of Michelbach, and the German soldiers led us to a home that was their Company Headquarters. We were placed along a fence and were told to sit down. One by one they took us in to be interrogated.

When the guards were not looking, I took some letters and other personal items I had on me and buried them in the dirt behind me. I did not want to give any helpful military information to the Germans. When my turn came, the guards marched me into a back room in the house and sat me on a kitchen chair. The German who did the interrogating spoke intelligible English. He was quick to point out who I was and with what division and company I served. I thought to myself, "I just got rid of some very precious letters, and I don't remember what else I buried."

A POW's Travels

The interrogator continued to seek information from me, but I said I was just a field medic and had no access to military information. I would continue to give just my name, rank, and serial number as we were all instructed to do. At one point, the interrogator blurted out that the war was going badly for them and that they were losing a lot of good soldiers. Without thinking, I replied, "Good," and for that the guard behind me gave a slug to the side of my head with a rifle butt. It stung for a moment, and then I was pulled up and marched out of the house. The guards again stood all of us up and started a second march back to what might have been their Division Headquarters where all of us had to be re-interrogated. This went just as quickly, and soon we were on the march again.

On this leg of our march, we encountered a couple of P47's returning from a raid. As they dove down toward our column, everyone made a leap for cover to the side of the road. Fortunately for us, they appeared to be out of ammunition, for the P47's then flew right back into the sky and kept on going.

An Upgrade in Status

When darkness arrived, we were led into a barn and waited there for some time. The doors of the barn opened, and guards with lanterns came in with an officer who proceeded to read off names.

The first name called out was 1st Lt. Jordan. He was led to the door behind the officer. The next name called out got no response because it was not understood. Again the name was called out, and again no response, so one of the guards came over and grabbed me by the arm and shouted at me for not understanding my own name. Whatever he was saying in German did not sound like Shier to me.

Lt. Jordan and I were taken away for further interrogations back to their Corps and Army Headquarters. I don't know where I slept that night, and I never heard what happened to the medics we left behind. (They were all released at the war's end.) I later learned that as a courtesy to all officers, an enlisted person was assigned as an aide. On the following morning, Lt. Jordan and I were escorted to Army Headquarters by a German soldier driving a Mercedes convertible.

We were led into a back room of a farmhouse that served as an office. A German general in a tattered gray uniform proceeded to ask questions of Lt. Jordan through an interpreter. It turns out that the general was the chief medical officer of the Corps area and only wanted to discuss the latest medical information. After this latest questioning, we were never bothered by any Germans seeking military information. The comment I heard was, "They are only medics. What do they know?"

The New POW Routine

That evening we were marched to a farmhouse leading out of town. This was where we met up with a small company of German soldiers that escorted prisoners back to the Prisoner of War camps. Lt. Jordan and I joined five other POWs already traveling with about twenty-five Wehrmacht soldiers in this small company. The other POWs were a captain and lieutenant from the Royal Air

Force, two noncom airmen from the 8th Air Force, and one other GI from the 7th Army who had escaped from a POW camp and had been recaptured.

The next two weeks were spent marching to the rear at night to avoid strafing by U.S. Army planes. Our daylight hours were spent in barns of any farm that was along our path of retreat. This is when I would try to cleanup and get some sleep. I marveled at how these old soldiers of the Wehrmacht could keep up the nightly march with the little rest they received. My amazement of these men was, because they were so old, they were kept from the front lines. All of them were in their early to late 40s. Some of them did not even bother to carry weapons, and others had rifles with broken bolts and stocks. All of their food and other supplies were carried on a horse drawn flatbed carriage from World War I.

When we marched at night, the German soldiers would take turns getting onto the carriage for a rest because once the troops got started at night, there was no stopping until morning daylight. On one such night, I had the need to relieve myself and finally convinced the one English speaking guard to let me drop out of the column and urinate down the side of the mountain we were on. As bad as I had to go, I was still too slow for the guard left behind to watch me. The guard was losing sight of the column in the darkness, and he, like me, was afraid to be left behind. So he poked me with his rifle butt, and said, "March or else." Well, I wasn't finished, but wet pants were better than a bullet to the head.

Some nights it was so dark I was afraid to take one step in front of me, and on other nights there might be a full moon that lit up the valleys below or the mountain peaks on which I walked. The area I was in and the conditions around me would not even let me consider a possible escape. To help ease the tension of these nights, I started singing as I was being marched back, and for some unknown reason, the guards never told me to stop. My fellow prisoners and some of the German guards did comment on my singing, saying I was flat or a miserable monotone, but never directed me to stop. One evening I was crossing over a large stone bridge that was still intact, and I asked the English speaking guard if he knew the name of the large river, and I was told it was the Danube.

One evening after that crossing, we had to pass through a city that was still active with a large population. The officers found a "breu haus" open and got the okay for the guards and prisoners to go in for a drink. Not everyone went in, but I did, and the first thing I was asked was if I was a "flieger" (air force member). I quickly said, "Nein" because we had heard that at one time or another if the civilians got to a downed air force person first, he might be killed on sight. The second question for me was did I have any money to pay for a drink. I dug into my pocket and pulled out some army marks issued to me, and to my surprise, the waitress accepted them. "War is hell" — and also very strange.

During the daylight hours, the Germans continued to hide out in various barns they commandeered from local farmers. Since there were so few of us prisoners, the Germans fed us whatever they were having. This was one meal a day of a watery potato soup with some kind of greens in it with a pork bone to give it a little flavor. They picked up loaves of black bread as we marched along, but I never saw from where. Each of us received a quarter loaf each day that I would munch on as the day went on. One day the Germans found a stash of Swiss chocolates and Schnapps. I received one piece of the chocolate, but they kept the drinks for themselves.

One of the hardships the other prisoners and I had to endure was the cool spring temperatures and how to keep warm. One of the things to which we resorted was sleeping near or on the manure piles in the barns. Thus, in the afternoon when it warmed up a bit, the others and I would strip down to our waists. We would air out our clothes and check for ticks. We had found them on our bodies several times in the past.

On the first Sunday after my capture, I sighted a church near where we had stopped for the day. I asked if it was a Catholic church and was told that is was. So I continued to inquire if it would be possible for me to attend a service there. The shocked response was that they did not want to have the enemy sitting next to them in "their" church. This was a strange and upsetting reply to me, but in retrospect I think I would feel the same.

The next week passed quickly, and the pace for our German guards was more intense. This was due to the speedy advancement of Allied troops deeper into Germany. Now they feared capture themselves. I heard that several times in the past couple of days the Wehrmacht officer who had charge of us was in contact with some German SS soldiers. They insisted that all seven POWs be turned over to them for execution. Our officer guard was just as insistent that all of the POWs were his responsibility, and he was not giving them up to anyone except the Camp Commandant. I later learned that the real reason we were kept from the SS Nazi Special Police soldiers was the officer guard wanted some security. All of us would be used as hostages to bargain with when we ran into the Allied troops.

On Monday, April 30, 1945, the other prisoners and I were told that this was the end of the run. Our German guards learned that the Russian troops were a short distance to the east of our location and were making arrangements to surrender. Lt. Jordan and the British officers said they would accept the surrender of the Germans, but the German officer wanted more security for his men and himself.

The Surrender Happens

After some discussion, it was agreed that a Polish POW that was working the farm would go out and make contact with the closest Allied troops. This turned out to be the Third Division of the U.S. 7th Army. They arrived the next morning, Tuesday, May 1, 1945, to complete the surrender of our German guards to myself and the other POWs. I know that the Germans would not surrender to the seven POWs until the other Americans arrived to back us up, but the fear of being a Russian prisoner made the surrender a reality. I consider this moment the craziest of the war in which I served.

With great relief the troops of the Third Division took the Germans off our hands and marched them away. They also provided us with a 2 1/2-ton army truck to transport us back to the nearest camp for repatriated prisoners. That camp was at Mannheim, Germany. It would take us all day to drive the more than 200 miles from the small village of Biberg, Germany, where I was repatriated back to the camp. This was about thirty miles southeast of Munich that we drove through until we came to Dachau, the death camp northwest of Munich. The driver of the transport truck asked if it would be okay to stop there for a few minutes. The Dachau camp was just liberated the day before.

The Grizzly Picture

The driver stopped and parked on the street right in front of the main gate to the camp. Everyone jumped out of the truck and ran into the camp. I was still too terrified by the war and my recent experiences to do as they were doing. The war had not ended as yet, and I was always afraid of another desperate counterattack by the Germans. When my companions did not come right out from the camp, I got out myself and walked over near the gate. I looked down the iron fence to my left and saw their thin, unmoving arms extended from behind the fence. I moved over for a closer look and was horrified to see that these skeletons were alive. My heart began to ache, and tears started to well up in my eyes. To this day, I see the sunken eyes in their meatless skulls and wonder, "How could one human do this to another?" The sight was so horrifying to me that I turned right around and got back into the truck.

There are some things from this war experience that no human should ever forget, and the memories of Dachau are too painful to talk about.

The Journey for Home Begins

After an hour or less, everyone left the Dachau camp and returned to the personnel truck. We continued our journey back to the ex-POW camp at Mannheim, Germany. The first order of business was to strip bare-naked in a large tent where we were cleaned up, deloused, and issued all new clothing. Everything that we were wearing was taken and burned. I was allowed to keep my dog tags, Red Cross arm band, plastic covered ID card and my bandage shears. I also kept my prayer book and medical folder.

When we had completed dressing, we were escorted to an old German barracks. I took the first open bunk, stored my belongings and headed for the mess hall. The food was great even if I don't recall what it was.

The next day, May 2, 1945, the other new arrivals and I had checkups for our general health and a visit to the dentist. From this day forward, my time was spent in the camp waiting for transportation assignments. The war was still on officially, so I stayed close to camp.

Five days later on May 7th, the camp was notified that the Germans had surrendered and the signing would be the next day. All those in camp had their own little way of celebrating, but most of it was just a lot of hollering and whooping it up. The lights came on in the cities and lit up the streets, and civilians appeared everywhere.

It was the second week at camp, and I had another brush with death. I was carrying one of the souvenir German pistols I had acquired from my former guards after my liberation. I took it out of my pocket to show a new replacement GI in the mess hall. When I let this green kid hold the pistol, he pulled the trigger. A 25 caliber slug whizzed right past my ear, hit the wall behind me, and then ricocheted around the dining room. I grabbed the pistol back and stood and shook for a few minutes, then thanked God no one was hit.

On May 16, 1945, I packed up my belongings and got ready to leave camp. To lighten my load, I sold off five of the relic pistols I had picked up from the German guards that held me. There were personnel troop trucks to transport all of us leaving for the airport. We boarded a DC-3 cargo plane and then took off for Le Havre, France. The plane was only equipped with metal bucket seats along each wall. We had a parachute for a seat cushion. This was to be my first airplane ride, and I experienced a little bit of stomach queasiness.

Soon into the flight, I fell asleep and missed the low fly-over of Paris, France, that the pilot provided. As soon as we landed in Le Havre, we were driven to the shipping docks where we boarded a converted Kaiser Liberty Ship. The name of the ship was the Wm. T. Berry, and it had the appearance of having survived the entire war. Its crew was merchant marines, but had a small group of navy seamen to man the guns onboard.

V. THE LONG VOYAGE HOME

You can close your eyes to reality but not to memories.

🖘 Lee

70 mm

Unknown to virtually everyone on the planet, J. Robert Oppenheimer had prepared isotopes of uranium-235 and plutonium-239 and had constructed the first atomic bomb. It would be tested on July 16, 1945 and then twice again, in August over Japan.

8 mm

Life on the High Seas Routine

The next morning, the ship set sail for Southampton, England, where the rest of the convoy would assemble. There were three hundred small canvas bunks stacked five high in the main hold. I was lucky enough to get a top bunk, making it easy for me to get in and out when I needed. Those below me really had a tough time if they tried to sleep on their sides. Once again I had to find something to do with my time besides eating and sleeping.

From May 18th to May 20th all of the convoy was set, and off we sailed across the North Atlantic heading toward Nova Scotia, Canada. The meals were absolutely the best that could be provided under these conditions. They included all the eggs and bacon or ham you could eat for breakfast. For lunch, great sandwiches with what I thought was fresh bread, but it came from a giant cooler. There was always fresh fruit and the biggest steaks for supper every day that we were out to sea.

The eating onboard had a regular schedule, and sleeping was as-needed. That left a lot of the day's 24 hours to fill in for the next two weeks. If you did not like to stroll around the decks or stare down into the engine room, you would read. There were also a few craps games going on in several corners of the ship's hold. For me the action was the card games. Somehow I managed to befriend some of the merchant seamen. I was allowed to join in the pinochle games that were going on in their mess room.

There were two large tables that sat six people each with a six-handed pinochle game being played. I would not get up from the table unless someone asked for a time-out to use the "head" or wanted to get something to eat. The complete time at sea, I probably slept no more than ten times on the whole trip. A few days out to sea, I learned that there was a small infirmary onboard with four hospital bunks in it. When I needed to catch a few minutes of sleep, I snuck into the infirmary and used one of the bunks.

The card games were played with two pinochle decks minus the nine cards. We had three sets of partners at each table. It took me a few games to catch on and master the shuffling of two decks. In my youth at home, I played pinochle at the age of twelve. This was a lot more challenging, plus a lot more fun. I do not recall what stakes we played for, but I must have been able to handle it. This is mentioned here because there were $3,000 bucks in some craps game jackpots.

Getting the Good News at Sea

A week out to sea we received word that the last of the U-Boats had been accounted for. With this news, the convoy was allowed to turn on the running lights of all the ships and break radio silence. The way the ships were strung out with lights on made the high seas looked like Broadway in New York City. This was a great look with the lights on the shimmering waters.

The convoy continued its path through the North Atlantic, riding the rough seas. It was hard to believe how well I rode out the trip on this small freighter. One of the days when the seas were particularly rough, I stood at the bow of the ship to ride out the waves. There were a couple of days when the swells were twenty to thirty feet deep, but these were easily handled by the others and me.

The card games and the great meals continued. It really felt great to be free and on our way home. One thing on the downside was my being taken aside by one of the officers to inform me that I would no longer be allowed to sneak into the sickbay. I had been using one of the nice, plush bunks to catch up on my sleep. So for the last couple of nights at sea, I would have to climb up to the sagging canvas bunk. This was only attempted if I was too tired to stand up.

About one day out at sea after sunset, I was able to see the lights from the Canadian shoreline. As the convoy sailed just off the coastline, I was able to make out more familiar landmarks. The ships passed by Long Island and New York City on to the final port in New Jersey. The ships pulled up to the docks at Camp Kilmer and one by one started to unload the returning ex-POWs. We were directed to waiting 2 1/2-ton personnel trucks that would bring us into camp.

The day was June 4, 1945, ending seventeen days at sea.

The first thing the GI's did after their barracks were assigned was to race for the nearest telephones to call home. Although I was anxious to call my family in Detroit, I waited till evening when the coin telephones would be available. When I finally got through to my home, my mother took the call. She was shocked to hear my voice, since she had not received the telegram of my repatriation. The balance of our conversation consisted of my mother continually asking if I was okay and how I was feeling. After saying hello to the rest of the family, I stated I would be home in a few days.

The next day the other ex-POWs and I boarded trains to military installations where all would receive their orders for two months of R&R furlough time. On the second day of my train ride, I arrived at Ft. Sheridan, Illinois. Everyone receiving the special R&R was again checked over and received orders and ration coupons. Also included were transportation tickets to our homes and our next destination. Not all of the R&R days at home were the same. Mine was for 66 days, plus days for traveling home and to my next assignment. I boarded the train at Ft. Sheridan on June 8, 1945, and did not have to be at Hot Springs, Arkansas until August 15, 1945.

It was a long train ride back to Detroit as the train made many local stops with this run. As the train was pulling into Michigan Central Depot, I walked to the end of the railroad car to secure my duffel bag and stood at the door to be the first to exit the train. This being my third trip to the depot, I knew which streetcars and buses to board for a quick ride home. The next couple of days were spent visiting immediate family and close-by relatives. They quickly got over their interest in my war stories, and I started visiting all the service clubs and enjoying any freebies for someone in uniform.

Most of my activities centered on the theaters during the afternoon hours. The beaches and the parks with the many rides and attractions did not interest me. In the evenings, I headed to downtown Detroit to visit all the great night spots and clubs. I would listen to the local bands and combos playing. Of course, there were many neighborhood clubs like the Vogue Show Bar and the Conner Show Bar with musicians who excelled. These were the two of many that I frequented from dozens that were available each night.

Sixty-Six Days in Detroit

The downtown YMCA and the USO club were my favorite spots for dancing when a date wasn't available. For me, that was most of the time. When I had a companion with me, it usually was one of my younger aunts or a girlfriend of one of the fellow servicemen that hung out with the corner soda shop gang before the war. The summer passed quickly, and before I knew it, my sixty-six-day leave was ending. All of the talk now was of ending the war with Japan and who might be shipping out to that zone.

On the morning of August 14, 1945, I headed to the Michigan Central Depot and boarded a train for Chicago, Illinois. In Chicago, I transferred to the high speed Blue Diamond line, making for a quick trip to St. Louis Missouri, traveling at speeds of over ninety miles per hour. The final leg of my trip to Hot Springs, Arkansas, was by bus. The Missouri-Pacific Transportation Co. was not a fast-mover as the previous carrier and seemed to find all of the back roads. My days of traveling were rapidly coming to an end as we reached Little Rock, Arkansas. When the bus reached downtown, the streets were packed with people yelling and cheering. The driver had to slow down till he reached the bus terminal. It was then that we heard the good news that Japan had surrendered. Some of the other passengers were also servicemen, and they spoke of leaving the bus to join the celebration. After some thought on the matter, we all agreed to stay on the bus and continue our trip to Hot Springs.

The other servicemen and I arrived at our destination in time to meet the August 15th deadline. My room at the Arlington Hotel was ready for me, and a schedule of the required meetings and activities was made available to everyone for the rest of our stay. The next two weeks would be at the Arlington Hotel where the other ex-POWs and I had access to the Hot Springs spa, plus the in-house entertainment clubs. They provided a continual routine of meals, local sight-seeing trips, a jukebox that never stopped playing, and female escorts.

Of all the GI's with me here at the hotel, I never did get close to any of the guys with whom I hung out. This was also the case with the young ladies from the different USO's and church groups that would visit with all of us. I often wondered if there was some kind of marking on my forehead that alerted all the females to steer clear of me. There was never anytime in my two years in uniform that I had what one could call a real date.

The two weeks at the Arlington Hotel passed quickly, and I was on my way to Camp Crowder, Missouri. This was the center for reassigning ex-POWs while they finish out their service time. The current rule was that no ex-POWs could be returned to a combat location unless they asked or volunteered for it.

The stay at Camp Crowder was less than three weeks, but was uneventful with one exception. On the second weekend at camp, a group got together for a trip into town. It was a Friday night. One of the servicemen in my barracks had a 1940 Plymouth sedan with him in camp. Six of us piled into the car and headed into town to an upscale restaurant for dinner. I was nineteen and never was a "drinker" of any kind. I tried a bottle of beer, which I finished even though it tasted bitter to me. We left the diner and headed for a show club that also had dancing. I do not know if we were still in Missouri or had driven to another state. I bring this up because there was a bottle of whiskey on the table, and we had to purchase our own mix and soft drinks separately.

After my experience with the bitter beer taste from dinner, I ordered a glass of Coca-Cola. As the evening wore on, I started getting light headed and in a few hours really felt sick.

The party ended soon after my complaints, and we started back to camp. I do not remember walking to the car, so they probably helped me along. Sometime during the trip back to camp, I came to with my head out the window. I was heaving so violently that the spray covered the entire side of the car. The next time I came to I was being dragged up the stairs to the second floor of the barracks. I could not say if this was late Friday night or early Saturday morning.

The Naive Kid from Detroit Lives

The next time I awoke, it was Sunday noon, and I was choking. I had slept through Saturday. What a shock this was to me! I was flat on my back and still dressed in my uniform from Friday night. Before I made a move, I smelled a terrible stench. It was my vomit, and I was lying in it. It almost covered my entire face. If they had lain me on my side or my stomach, I would have been dead. After I cleaned up both myself and the bunk, I started asking questions. The naive kid from Detroit did not realize it, but these so-called fellow warriors were spiking my Coke with shots of Imperial all night long on Friday.

As a nondrinker, I was again very close to death. I felt more alone than ever and longed to be home with my family. This is very odd because our family did not do a lot of things together, but we were still close. (After I married and had children of my own, I changed this for the better.)

On September 20, 1945, I received word that I would be assigned to Percy Jones Hospital in Battle Creek, Michigan. As a medic, it was decided I would work in a medical facility. Four of the former ex-POWs from the Detroit area were given our papers, and we shipped out the next day as a group. On the train ride to Battle Creek, we noticed our travel papers did not indicate an arrival time. All agreed that we would continue past Battle Creek and return to Detroit.

Making My Move for Growth

When we arrived in Detroit, Michigan, the plan was to meet in two weeks, then drive back to Battle Creek. One of the servicemen would pick up his car from home, and we would travel back together on October 4, 1945.

Late on the evening of October 4th, we reported to the nighttime officer in charge at the hospital. He informed us that he was not ready with our assignments and was looking for something to do with the four of us. Showing a smile on his face, he randomly asked when we had last been on a furlough. All of us in unison said it had been a while.

So with that, the Officer of the Day signed all four of us up for a two-week leave at home. After a few minutes, the paper work was ready, and we were back on the way to Detroit. On October 18, 1945, the four of us again reported to Percy Jones Hospital and received our work assignments. The assignment for me was as an orderly and assistant when a nurse was in need of help. This was in a locked ward on the third floor of the hospital. Most of the patients had mental problems due to head wounds received in battle. Some patients were alcoholics, and others had a wide range of mental problems, discovered after the GI had been inducted or enlisted into the army. This ward also was the collection area for unusual cases that needed special attention. Two of these were wheelchair polio cases, and another was a suicidal patient. He had jumped off an apartment roof, but at the last second reached out to grab a high tension wire. The high voltage was enough to burn off both of his hands.

Those of us that worked on this ward entered the locked area with someone covering our backs. I worked with this daytime crew for a couple of months.

The Daily Routine

Other than the regular routine of taking patients to doctor visits in other parts of the hospital or helping them in the restroom, things would be calm. Then there was the rare occasion when a patient would snap.

Everyone on duty had to jump in and help. At 175 pounds and 5 feet 11 inches, it was my job on these emergencies to jump onto the bed with the patient to secure his arms and legs. I would literally wrestle him down with a bear hug and hold him as still as possible while the nurse sedated him with a syringe injection.

On another occasion, the alcoholic who had pass privileges went off the wagon at a tavern close to the hospital. It took six MP's to drag him back to the hospital and get him into a padded cell. While trying to get him sedated, he was literally flinging these six heavyweights into the air. They would jump right back on him until he was too tired or maybe was just ready to give up. Once they had this patient sedated and into a strait jacket, we would leave and nurse our sore, aching bones.

On most occasions when a patient got testy, I or another medic and even a nurse that was available would just talk till the patient settled down. My work schedule was for twelve hours on duty and twelve hours off. This was 7:00 a.m. till 7:00 p.m. for all personnel at the hospital. The hospital was connected to all of the service, maintenance areas, garages, and billeting apartments by long service tunnels. These connecting tunnels served me well because it permitted me to go back and forth in the cold weather. My living quarters were a large second floor room in a connected ten-room home. All I needed was a place to wash up and a bunk to sleep in.

There was no manual labor for the GI's at the hospital. The cleaning, cooking, and serving in the cafeteria was handled by the German POWs that were brought in from Ft. Custer every day.

The Start of a New Direction

It was at this time in my life that I started attending church services on the mezzanine at the hospital entrance. There was also a small theater in the hospital for movies and occasionally a musical show. If it was dancing I wanted, I would go downtown to the Tropics Club and show bar. When I was on the Rhine River for the Christmas of 1944 along with many of my comrades, I had made the pledge to be home for Christmas of 1945.

The approval for my extended pass came through, and I was on my way home to spend Christmas with my family. Before the holiday ended, I was invited to a New Year's Eve party in Hamtramck. The party was uneventful, but lasted till daylight the next morning. My trip to the party was by streetcar and bus changes. As I was leaving the party, a sailor who had his father's 1940 Dodge, was also leaving. The sailor was as sober as I was because neither of us was brave enough to take any alcoholic drinks. He was hesitant to give me a lift until he saw that I was also sober.

There was heavy frost on all the car windows, so he was only able to scratch out a little four by eight inch spot. There was nowhere for me to see through. We turned off of Charest Street onto Caniff Street heading west. I said it would be okay to drop me off at Jos. Campau to catch the streetcar. Just as I said that, a streetcar passed through the intersection. Being a nice guy, he said he was going to turn the corner and catch that streetcar for me.

When I regained consciousness, I was being set down on the sidewalk by several bystanders who had carried me out of the wrecked Dodge. I turned my head a bit and saw the sailor sitting on the curb and sobbing into his hands.

When I looked the other way, there was the wrecked car halfway through the double front doors of the Cunningham Drugstore at the southeast corner of Jos. Campau and Caniff. Before I could say anything, the ambulance pulled up, placed me on a stretcher, and drove to St. Francis Hospital in Hamtramck.

My face was bloody and full of glass from going through the windshield, and my left arm was sprained, but no fractures. A nurse spent over two hours removing glass from my face, cleaning up some of the bloody abrasions, and then putting my arm in a sling. I do not remember how I went home, but I think I took a taxicab from the hospital. That evening, after a rest and cleaning most of the blood from my uniform, I took off for the Vanity Ballroom for a night of dancing. The sling on the arm and the patched up face did not turn away the young ladies from dancing with me. Maybe they just assumed they were war wounds.

The next day my furlough was up, and I returned to Battle Creek. When my C.O. saw me, he immediately assigned me to the afternoon shift. He did not want me trying to lift or subdue patients. The hours were now 7:00 p.m. to 7:00 a.m., but still in the locked ward. I would work two days, then receive two days off. This new arrangement allowed me to take off for home in Detroit. As soon as my shift ended at 7:00 a.m., I flew out the door of the hospital and headed for U.S. 12. I was always lucky enough to hitch a ride back home. This proved to be the best deal for me since I was still in uniform.

To make sure I was back at the hospital for my next shift, I would ride the Michigan Central train back to Battle Creek. The fare for a round trip was three dollars, and when I turned in the unused half, I received a buck and a half to use toward my next ticket.

When I was staying at the hospital, my routine went something like this: Get an early supper and be on the ward by 7:00 p.m., then I would review with the head nurse to see if there were any changes I needed to know.

My new duties for the shift that extended past midnight to 7:00 a.m. had me working alone on this secured ward. The main duty now consisted of bed check, with a late night drink and snack for patients before lights out. This was usually around 10:00 p.m. with a W.A.C. helping me with the patients who were confined to bed.

Once the lights were out, the door was secured, and I would take up my post in the ward office. Every couple of hours I would take a stroll through the ward, checking to see that everyone was resting well. Then it was back to the office to continue reading one of the many paperback novels and books that were available. I was able to read one complete book every two or three nights. The sad note here is that I am unable to recall one title of the many novels I read at this time.

When my shift ended at 7:00 a.m., I would go to the mess hall for breakfast and then to my bunk room. If I was going home, I would head out the front door of the hospital and rush to U.S. 12 to hitch a ride home. The days I stayed in Battle Creek on my days off, I would stroll into town for a movie or window shop for a few hours. In the evening, I would join the other workers from my ward at the Tropics Club. It's amazing to me the number of show bars and dancing saloons and clubs, and how many musicians were available. One out of every hundred in town must have played in a band. I never tired of going to the clubs to be entertained by the great music. As time went on, my shyness dissolved enough to let me ask the young ladies to dance, but not too often.

The routine at the hospital continued through the winter and most of the spring of 1946. In March when I was home for two days, I was drawn to the old German Deutsches Haus. Now it was the CYO center for Catholic Youth activities. Before I was called into the service, I had spent some time at this center. Although there isn't proof of the date, I believe it to be March 14, 1946. The CYO was presenting Lenten talks in the evening with snacks and jukebox music afterwards. A charming young lady and her friend caught my eye as they danced to the music. When they approached the jukebox to make a new selection, I stepped up to them and initiated a conversation. After this moment we would spend a lot of time together.

There were light talks, some dancing, and after that, I would walk the two of them home. From this day forward, I would come back to Detroit on my days off. I soon found myself strongly attracted to the shorter and more reserved of the two. In two weeks time, I had fallen in love, and my family members were asking me why I had gone weird on them.

The Final Days in Battle Creek

I continued to spend all my non-working hours traveling to Detroit in hopes of running into the new love of my life. Near the end of April 1946, the list of those eligible for discharge on the first of the month came around. My name was not on it, although I had enough points to be discharged. I headed immediately to the personnel office to discuss correcting the list to include my name. After some discussion, the officer agreed with my count of the needed points. I spent the last week of April 1946 getting my work area in order and all of the paperwork completed.

The night before our exit of Percy Jones Hospital and Battle Creek, all of us in my group went downtown to celebrate. We had dinner together and then visited a few of our favorite night spots. At about 10:00 p.m., we left the last location and congregated on the sidewalk to say our last goodbyes to each other. In a couple of minutes, two MP's drove to us and stated we were under arrest. In unison we all stammered, "What is the problem?" They replied that we were all out of uniform and that our hats were on our belts instead of our heads.

No amount of explaining that we had only moments before stepped on the sidewalk and were engrossed in our goodbyes could sway the MP's. Their reply was that they were ordered to crack down on the uniform problem and pile us into the command car that took us to the Ft. Custer detention center. After a few hours and a discussion with the officer of the day, he okayed our release when learning of the circumstances and that we were being discharged the next day. I was, to say the least, mildly ticked off that my last night in town was spent in the lockup. Although it was a short stay and of no consequence, I wondered if this was payback for any of my earlier indiscretions.

VI. PEACE

Around every person is a sphere of influence beyond which he cannot pass, but within range of that circle, he is powerful and free.

ഴ Anonymous

70 mm

War over and millions of veterans home starting families and buying homes and starting delayed careers, the United States experienced twenty years of unprecedented economic success. No nation on earth has ever equaled the improvement of lifestyle experienced from 1945 through 1965.

8 mm

The Conclusion

O n May 1st, I received my discharge, ending my World War II service. I raced to the Metro with my ticket for home! The transfer to the train home was swift. My first action at home was to call Margo and make a date. After three years of dating, we were finally married. The date was May 21, 1949. That was six months after she persuaded me to apply for a job with Michigan Bell Telephone Company. In 1951, the first of our four children arrived. There's Kathy Ann, Kerry William, Kitty Marie, and finally in 1960 we had Kelly Michael.

All the time these moments were going on in my life,

I pursued another goal, that being the continuing pursuit of my education. Because the daylight hours were for work, I started night classes at our local high school. This continued until I had enough credits to receive my high school diploma. When I interviewed for my job at Michigan Bell, I was told that the diploma was not needed (now a college degree is required for my job). In 2001, at the age of seventy-five years, I proudly walked out onto the stage of Anchor Bay High School to receive my diploma! Amid the cheers of my children and grandchildren, Kathy Ann, my oldest who is a student counselor in that system, pushed me to complete the dream when she learned that I did not have the diploma. I also found it necessary to attend college courses to keep up with the different aspects of my job.

Margo and I did not have to push too hard with our children when it came to their own education. They just took a good look at their own parents.

They have all gone on to successful careers, followed by wonderful marriage partners. Margo and I have nine grandchildren with four already married, and five great-granddaughters. With just under thirty-four years of service at Bell, I retired in 1982.

We have traveled over forty-five of our Great States and have made several trips to Europe.

Now in my eighties, I see how my war experience directed my outlook on life and left me the luckiest husband and father on earth.

Margo enjoys a great summer day riding with Bill in his first car — a 1937 Ford

Margo Easthope and Bill in 1946

Bill and Margo Shier on the occasion of their 50th
Anniversary, May 21, 1999

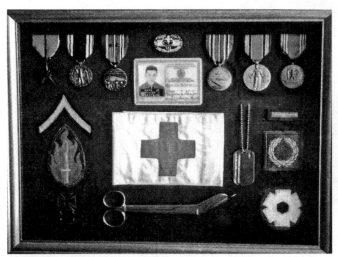

Medals and treasures from Bill Shier's Escapes and
Escapades: The Bronze Star, POW Medal, Euro-Campaign
with 2 Stars, Combat Medic, American Campaign, Victory
Medal, Good Conduct Medal, Medic I.D., Medic Arm Band,
Scissors, Dog Tags, PFC Stripe, Sharpshooter award, Six
Month Overseas Service, Discharge Ribbon, 6th Army
Corps, 63rd Division patch

Bill and Margo with their 9 grand children, May 21, 1999

Bill and Margo with their family, May 21, 1999

Kitty, Kathy, Margo and Bill, Kelly and Kerry, May 21, 1999

school board candidates think? Look inside today's Voice.

50¢ AT NEWSSTANDS

The Bay VOICE

A Weekly Newspaper Serving Chesterfield, New Baltimore and the Anchor Bay Area

Look for a special section with lots of information on New Baltimore's Bay-Rama festival inside today's Voice. The event is June 13-17.

June 6, 2001 ■ Vol. XVII No. 23

Fifty-six years later; WWII vet gets diploma

Shier, 75, will graduate with Anchor Bay Adult Education class June 7

BY JOE GRAY
VOICE STAFF WRITER

William Shier, 75, has his first paycheck, ticket stubs from every movie he has ever seen and a letter sent to his mother stating he was missing in action during World War II.

His paper trail is a testament to the history that he has lived.

Now, he is about to add one more scrap of memories to his collection — a high school diploma.

He will join 41 other Anchor Bay Adult Education graduates at commencement June 7.

Shier raised four children, took college courses, worked 35 years for Michigan Bell and saw the birth of nine grandchildren without the distinction of being a high school graduate.

"I was never embarrassed," he said from his Clinton Township home. "But, getting the diploma is a matter of pride."

Shier said things were different when he got out of the army in 1946.

"You didn't need a diploma to get a good job," he explained.

When Shier got out of the army, he went to work for Michigan Bell and they didn't require him to finish high school. He dropped out of school after the tenth grade to work during the booming wartime economy. He took night school courses until he was drafted in 1944. Shier married Margaret in 1949 and raised their children — Kathy, Kerry, Kitty and Kelly — and never told them their father

didn't finish high school.

"It never came up, because it didn't really matter," Margaret said. "He took classes in college, but he never got around to getting his high school diploma."

Above, William Shier as he looked in Europe during World War II. Left, at his Clinton Township home proudly showing war medals and a scrapbook.

Over the years, Shier has taken English, writing and history classes at Wayne State University, Detroit Mercy and Macomb

Continued on page 2

WWII

Continued from page 1

Community College without earning college credit.

Around five years ago, he tried to get a degree from another district. He took his paperwork in, but was denied because he needed a first-aid class to complete the requirements.

"I dropped it, because I wasn't going back to school," he said.

What Shier didn't realize, his army discharge papers stated he had the proper medical training to pass the requirement, but he never showed the district the papers.

Then his daughter, Kathy Nussman — a counselor at Lighthouse Middle School — got involved and presented her father's credentials to Anchor Bay. She got him the chance to walk across the stage nearly 50 years after his last high school class.

While Shier may rank his commencement as one of his most prideful memories, it will fall far from his most emotional.

During the war, two events had great impact on Shier. He was taken prisoner by the Germans and he paid a horrifying visit to the Dachau concentration camp.

"I'll never get that vision out of my mind," he said of the sight. He thought the prisoners were dead when he first approached the camp and saw their thin, unmoving arms extended from behind the fence.

He doesn't like talking about Dachau because of the painful memories.

"I can't talk about it for too long, because it brings tears to my eyes," he said.

Shier was also a prisoner of war for 16 days. It was near the end of the war and he was in a Jeep with six other soldiers and noticed four German soldiers washing in a horse trough near a farmhouse. At that time, German soldiers were just putting down their weapons and surrendering to Americans, so he figured it was a chance "for a medic to get some prisoners of war."

However, these soldiers ran into the house and returned with several other soldiers, who were firing machine guns at Shier and his group. The men were captured with no casualties.

"It was the end of the war, so I thought they had no reason to keep us alive," Shier said. "I thought they were going to kill us. I was really scared."

The Germans didn't kill their captives, instead they marched them around 200 miles toward the Russian front. Once the group got near the front, the Germans realized they would either have to surrender to the Americans or the Russians. They decided the Americans would protect them, so the Germans turned their weapons over and they became the prisoners.

Shier earned several commendations during his time in the army, including a Combat Medic Badge, Prisoner of War Medal, European Theater Operations Medal and the Bronze Star for heroism.

Shier carried a wounded American soldier who was under sniper fire to safety.

He has seen much and accomplished a lot in his life. Some of what he has done even outweighs the importance of the diploma he will be getting. But, he will gladly accept another "piece of paper" and add it to the memories because, he said, "this is just another step in my life."

WILLIAM J SHIER JR

To you who answered the call of your country and served in its Armed Forces to bring about the total defeat of the enemy, I extend the heartfelt thanks of a grateful Nation. As one of the Nation's finest, you undertook the most severe task one can be called upon to perform. Because you demonstrated the fortitude, resourcefulness and calm judgment necessary to carry out that task, we now look to you for leadership and example in further exalting our country in peace.

Harry Truman

THE WHITE HOUSE

APPENDIX

Civilian and Military Abbreviations Used in Escapes and Escapades

40x8 – Rail car definition meaning room for forty people or eight horses
Bn. – Battalion
Capt. – Captain, Officer rank
Co. – Company
C.O. – Commanding Officer
CYO – Catholic Youth Organization
Cpl. – Corporal – enlisted rank
GI – Government Issue (or, military person)
Lt. – Lieutenant, Officer rank
M.C. – Medical Corps
mm – millimeter
MP – Military Police
POE – Port of embarkation
POW – Prisoner of War
SS (Schutzstaffel) – quasi-military unit of the Nazi Party
U-Boats – German Submarines
U.S.O. – United Service Organization
W.A.C. – Woman Army Corps
YMCA – Young Men's Christian Association

ABOUT THE AUTHOR

Bill Shier worked for Michigan Bell Telephone Co. beginning in October of 1948. Thirty of these years were as a communications consultant starting with small businesses then ending with Government Agencies, including Post Offices and Military Bases.

Bill worked his way up the company ladder starting as a splicers helper, then to transportation, coin collecting and coin sales. After just under thiry-four years of exemplary service and being referred to as Mr. Telephone, Bill finally hung up the phone in August of 1982.

As noted in his book, he never had what was called a real date before meeting his future wife. He was very shy and introverted, but surviving his WWII service changed his whole life around.

Before the war, during the war, and after the war, Bill continued his fascination for the movies, but more so for the swing music of his youth. More time was spent at the many dance halls on the base service clubs or those in the Detroit Metro area.

It was on one of these dances that Bill spotted his wife-to-be. He still claims today that is was love at first sight. When the family came along after their marriage, Bill helped out at his son's little league baseball games and chaperoned the Cub Scouts. Bill also was on the Church committee helping to write the duties of the new Church Council.

Bill's retirement allowed him and his wife, Margo, to continue their world travels, including visiting forty-seven of our great fifty states. One which was Minnesota for the 35th reunion of his WWII Army Division.

Bill and Margo in Cape Cod, Massachusetts, for St. Vincent DePaul Society's National Conference in September, 1982

Margo and Bill have raised four children, and are enjoying nine grandchildren, four of whom are married, giving them five great-granddaughters. Next year, in 2009, they will celebrate their 60th wedding anniversary. Their future plans are to spend the rest of their eighties and maybe even some nineties at their summer place in Hillsdale, Michigan.